73

LOVE ENDS IN
A TANDEM KAYAK

Derrick C. Brown

Write Bloody Publishing
www.writebloody.com

First edition.
ISBN: 978-0-9842515-8-2

Cover Design by Angelo Maneage
Interior Layout by Angelo Maneage & Derrick C. Brown
Edited by Courtney Leblanc, Aly Sarafa and Wess Mongo Jolley
Proofread by Wess Mongo Jolley, Aly Sarafa and Sam Preminger
Author Photo by Noyel Gallimore

Type set in Bergamo.

Printed in the USA

Write Bloody Publishing
Los Angeles, CA

Support Independent Presses
www.writebloody.com

For Pops.

Dad: *Son, you should dedicate your poetry book to the Lord.*
Me: *Why would I ever want to do that?*
Dad: *So He may richly bless you.*
Me: *That's not the kind of love I want… do you think it could help sales?*

LOVE ENDS IN A TANDEM KAYAK

CONTENTS

CHAPTER WHERE THE AUTHOR REMEMBERS WHAT HE IS HERE FOR

CHAPTER WHERE THE AUTHOR MURDERS THE MIDNIGHT JEWELER

CHAPTER WHERE THE AUTHOR GOES ALL IN AND PUTS HIS LAST FUCK TO GIVE IN THE JUKEBOX OF JO

♥

"Human existence is so fragile a thing and exposed to such dangers that I cannot love without trembling."

—Simone Weil

"Life is short. Stunt it."

—Stuntman Rod Kimble

CHAPTER WHERE THE AUTHOR REMEMBERS WHAT HE IS HERE FOR

END TIMES TIMELINE
for Jeremy Radin

It's the early 1970s.
I am born as a screaming kind of child. *Oh God, Oh God.*
Mom dips my pacifier in sherry.
I stop screaming. Wood paneling blurs.
I bliss out and forget the lonely rooms.

A preacher named Hal Lindsey publishes
The Late Great Planet Earth. It gathers the flock.
They swear the end is near and everything changes for us.

It's 1984 and Christ is coming to blow up the earth
as Madonna drops *Like a Virgin*.
I roll around in the dirt likeshe did at the MTV music awards.
I roll around alone singing out my need to be touched for the very first time.
I am eleven years old and recognize that
it would be nice to fall in love before The Rapture.
To ascend hand in hand and not show up at the gates solo like a nerd.

The Rapture screams... *Any day now.*
I repent constantly because it could end tomorrow.
Sorry for burning Buzzy's arm while practicing our illusions.
Sorry for the obsession of flicking my nipples under the sheets.
Sorry for wanting this earth to last. Please let me rise with everyone.
Why care about anything else but heaven? This is all going away soon.
We sold so much stuff or gave it away. The things I loved.

I am a forced minimalist, a scared kid.
Scared of sleeping with the light off,
scared to not sleep on the floor,
scared of being left in Mexico again.
Scared of my friends pinning me down
and burning my hair again. Scared of someone taking Woody Woodpecker.
The last year I'll feel comfortable talking to him
and having him teach me how to French kiss.

My parents watch 700 Club Christian News, and
the Trinity Broadcast network a lot. Lindsey is on all the time.
The Book of Revelation and its love of the coming apocalypse
gets real popular. Antichrist obsession rises. We will elevator to heaven soon.
I learn to jump my bike off a curb by myself.

Lindsey makes links between the Bible, modern materialism,
the distant Cold War, gas shortages, and Satanic rock and roll.

I have a crush on Alyssa Milano.
She is far, and it's what I want. I'll listen to whatever she likes.
I hope it's "Crazy for You."

After The Rapture, they said there would be a seven-year period,
the Great Tribulation: the Antichrist arises, tremendous persecution.
666 and everything falls apart.
I finally figure out how to reassemble Optimus Prime.
Then the battle of Armageddon happens.
All those who have ever lived will be assigned to either to heaven or hell.
We end.

Every believer in heaven forgets that
living in a constant state of wanting,
of scared readiness and hopeful waiting, delirious pre-worrying
is hell.

Parents split. The pressure of too many un-truths.
They should have never married. Plates stacked too high.
It may be why I'm not married to this day.
Nothing in the future can be proven false, but an eleven-year old could see it.
Magic fills a hole in us with either hope or deceit.

I am still waiting for a kind of believer.
Oh God, Oh God. My bed narrows each year.
Oh God, Oh God. I can't endure another bullshit meal of desire.
Oh God, Oh God. Don't let me get used to dining alone.
Every hairstyle at this party looks like the end of a rope.

I am still in the waiting rooms of love. I daydream. It is sherry.

The earth is reborn perfect. Clean people inhabit it.
Nothing is wrong. The weather is great.
The wind hollows out the canyon. There is no coupling.

One day, the inhabitants line up
to take turns walking off
a beautiful cliff.

A WETSUIT TOO TIGHT
for the kid

I remember my teen time as a wetsuit
I couldn't wait to peel out of. It never fit, and I looked bad in it.

Some kids fell under a spell of romance and lust early.
Seemed like everyone in love was a runaway.

I couldn't get anyone to take my virginity...
maybe because I played volleyball.

I also thought if I could ollie 180 on my skateboard
someone would find me very attractive.

Steve Martin on vinyl became my friend. Styled by Emo Phillips and Harpo.
The pillow over my head was my friend when my parents shattered nightly.

I have no lasting advice for you and your new world
except to tell you crumbs:

It all changes when you get a car and time.
It all changes when you realize love doesn't end in one person.

Your face
just gets better and better. At least more interesting. Broken in.

Now can be awful, but nothing is as awful
as back then.

It's hard to hold your mom's scared hand.
It's hard for you to see her love for you is all of Appalachia.

It's hard to smile on
when friends and fathers fade. Hard is good.

The best writers I know are lonely
and the best writers I know are trying not to be by writing.

Jot it all down sometimes,
and spend a lot of time farting around, not writing.

Chase stupidity and say, "We are having fun right now,"
when you're having fun.

Risk the platinum branding-irons
of heartbreak every time.

Learn the joy of some
and not all.

I have had some love. I have had some good times.
I have some friends and they have some love left for me.

Turn on your headlamp, roam, and illuminate
all that I missed.

FORTUNE TELLER

Everyone you fall for young
will move away.

So just stay indoors.
Lay in bed. Listen to the cars and days go by like someone hushing you.

Why get a bike?
It will only get stolen.

Why wear your good shirt out to the show and meet anyone?
Your heart will break at least five times.

Your heart will break for someone
with teeth sharp as dollhouse roof shingles.

Your heart will break for someone
with a Pacific-wide voice singing in your little shower.

Your heart will break unless you can show restraint
and keep from showing her your close-up magic.

Your heart will break for someone
who sleeps deep, safe with their leg on you.

Your heart will break when you forget
that no one is the end.

Break
and then laugh.

Tired parents used to laugh,
used to swear the clouds changed into animals.

PAIN TALENT

for the fat hands of Doctor Naren, D.D.S.

Every smile is a fingerprint.
Mine, busted at best.
Never wired for beauty.
I am often embarrassed
of laughing too big
and showing my fangs.
A smile like a miner's headlamp
flickering its last breaths.

My smile is crooked
'cause a dentist got mad at me
for crying too much when I was 7.
He loaded me up on eight shots
of Novocaine, and it killed
some face nerves. I smile like
a limping creep. Like there's something
I'm not saying. A hiding thing. Little bit
of front tooth dangling out
like a leg off a dock.

Spit it out. Okay.

A basketball coach in high school said
I should be a dentist
because I was very unpleasant. I was.

This poem is not about my smile anymore.

Teeth are the hardest things we carry.
So much dead stuff
ground to confetti between them
and turned into energy, pulverized.

I wonder if the people I've kissed
could feel that kind of history
as their tongue waltzed around the smashed pottery studio
of my mouth.

All my relationships are like hotels.
I'm so excited to get there
and then, after a few hours,
the room starts to look the same,
and I miss home.

In all my relationships, I am the dentist
with my fingers in your mouth.

Searching my vessel of breath.
Fingering the life in my death.

I want new teeth.

I think of all my dentists as paladins of ache
and never ask if they have any other skills or hobbies.
I hate seeing anyone as just a palace of pain.

But here we are, vulnerable in the anguish throne,
the sum of all our disasters.

LIQUIDATE THE WHOLE COB

I do not care about what you have overcome
or the enemies that could not be bested.

I do not care about the things you saw die
in the receding fields. Did you think of skinning them?

I do not care about your love for what you can't explain.
Invent an answer.

I do not care about your father's skill for tomatoes
or silent retreat. Tell me how you raised yourself.

I do not care what a sad salad reminds you of.
It's always your scattered, soggy father.

I do not care that flowers react to classical music.
We kill them too.

I do not care why you open the urns on stranger's mantles.
Ash is underwhelming. It's you, at your hottest.

I do not care that the humorless winter beach
is your mother pushing the shore away. I know you are the shore.

I do not care that you want to be better to get applause.
Success is hilarious.

I do not care about your hunger for thirty-dollar honey and French art pomp.
Cool is boring. Walmart is art. Every diner is a gallery of blue need.

I only care about the imagined serenity
of doing nothing with you.

You said you needed me,
and it felt as good as floss after corn.

THE HUNT

Darling, have you seen where the sex went?
The weird rough ones we kept in the medicine chest,
by the Icy Hot? I doubt someone came in and burgled it.

It was right here.

Can you look for the jar that hurts to open?
The one where "Razor Love" plays when you lift the lid.
The label has a naïve beach town image with instructions on
how to tank the future.

Was it left behind the couch
where your yellow sock
would cock
up on the armrest, legs spread, ready for lazy sweating?

Did it drop behind the fridge
along with the Post-It Note about how your body
is pretending to love its hungry, hollow womb?
Or is it in the envelope with the birthday card
where you joke about my beer belly?

Where is it, honey?

Cayucos.

MANSION APARTMENT SHACK HOUSE

I will be immortalized in a joke.

The sex was disappointing.
I could tell she was fantasizing about someone else
as her VR headset
kept smashing into my forehead.

She asked what sex was to me.
I said, "Let's write it down and read each other's answer."
She wrote: *exploration, freedom in soft pain and pleasure control.*
I wrote: *it's a nice little test drive.*

"Test drive?" she asked.
"Yeah. Could we do this for years and not bury the electricity?"

"Bye, Derrick. It always gets buried."

I am blessed with so much vanishing.
My favorite dance move is the French drop.
Lots changed. Lots went away.
Most kids are sober now.
Most playgrounds are too safe.
We are just stretched-out kids. Scar enthusiasts. Corduroy nerdburgers.

When I see a kid wearing glasses
I want to kidnap them
and hear them correct me about history and say
"...um, actually," then collapse in admiration.

I started wearing glasses this year
and realized that all the compliments
I gave for classy turtlenecks
were actually for neck braces.

I see myself so clearly. Finally.
I see the heavy,
down at my ankles now
pushing
squeezing from the pores of my skin
like a Play-Doh Fun Factory spaghetti party.

Glasses off.
All the little errors on my face, erased.
I'm something softer. White balance dream intro. Fantasy gloss.
I also see I fantasize about other lives but never unwrapped this one fully.

A different date. We played a game at the dining table.

She asked me if I liked MASH.
I said, "It was the greatest." I hummed "Suicide is Painless" and she was confused.
She asked if it was my favorite game.
I said, "What? War? The game of war where you become obedient and worth
    nothing, laugh your way to the futile end?"
She said, "No, the game. Mansion. Apartment. Shack. House
It's how you predict your Life partner, number of kids, job, salary, car,
and where you live."
"Oh."
The game gave the answers: Love of my life: MacGruber. Zero kids by birth–
One from kidnapping. Constant soldier. Unsustainable dreamer salary. Small truck.
Home where I will live out my life? Inside me.

Across the room, a newscaster with no hand-jewelry tells a boring story
about a family and holds back a high-tide of tears.

Me too. It's been a hard run.
The critics even tore apart my potential ideas.
Tell the critics I'll be gone soon.

All this work and worry, and when I'm an idea in ash
they will say, "Oh, he had that one joke and made me laugh slightly."
Dust soon. Cry in the dust too long and it's mud and it's so heavy.
I need to tell people crazy shit. Scary stuff.
Love people too early. It's so fun to yell when leaving a sushi restaurant,
"Thanks. So good. I love you."
Love is dumb adoration, it turns the lamps on by clapping.

Why do I want to do it with the lights on? Love is a democracy,
and democracy dies in darkness. I'm a generator. Not the nice, quiet kind.

My little cells are specialized to carry electricity.
My love is electricity. My touch is electricity.
My want is a place to put the light.

NIGHT SCHOOL

...and the number is 81 in 22 years of activity
I have learned so much. Scared to at first
I didn't have sex until I was 19
It started in that Fayetteville dive bar
maybe spanky's roadhouse
the bj
by that russian-sounding woman named nadia
and she was wearing a black lace top
and I was 19 and in the army and dorkified
and I thought she liked me and felt proud
and she asked if I wanted to make out in the back
and I imagined stacks of beer and trying out french kissing
and there was just a couch
and paper towels and rubbing alcohol waiting
and then the bartender
tried to charge me when nadia left. tried to. john with a camaro paid for me
and I felt a glacier rip into my hull.
and she ran out to me with her number, so I thought she liked me
and I called her days later to try and get a date
to prove to the other soldiers that she wasn't a sex worker
and she was always too busy for a date and said
I looked too much like a christian skateboarder
I was glad she gave me an actual number.
I'd leave long messages on her answering machine
pretending she was my girlfriend
one day she answered and told me I was too squeaky clean
and to have an extraordinary life.
I still left messages.

I am 19 in lancaster, ohio, flirting poorly and
getting ditched by my friends at a house party.
charles took my car for beers
and this was before cell phones
and I had my first sex experience
with a no surfing in hell t-shirt clumped in a ball
and flannel plaid pants around my ankles
and my dumb blue vans locking them in
and I loved it and she came and it was a surprise for both of us
and there were no doors in the trashed house
and she wanted to go again, so we did, and I told her I was a virgin
and she was sure I was lying

but I wasn't.
there was a gush
I thought the gush was pee
and it was something much more fun
and she was a mom, beaming, mom-beams, a moon from ohio
and the other soldiers
called me motherfucker for a week
and I loved it. I never got her last name.
and I slept in a basement alone
and wandered the city the following day
and found my car parked at a random house
and kicked charles hard, five times in the ribs for ditching me.
I said, you never leave a man behind even in ecstasy

I am 20. myrtle beach is a big tribal tattoo. a lost flip-flop.
I hooked up with a woman outside
the purple gator who claimed to be
journey front man steve perry's illegitimate road daughter,
a part-time stripper, very tan and forward, good forward
and the car was a red coupe and I'm too tall for a coupe
and we tried to fuck in the passenger side,
but it had bucket seats
which pulled her hips
dooooooooowwwwwwn and away from me, but we got there
and she finished and said she hated her boyfriend, *whaaaa?*
and she said he didn't love her the way she needed, but they needed each other
and I didn't understand for years what I was to people
and she said I was a good fling and I was funny
and I said we all need the clowns to make us laugh and it did not make her laugh
and I realized it's kind of beautiful to be a break from real life for someone,
a moment like a cologne, sprayed to mask bucket seat stink.

I was a born-again virgin for the next seven years.
it was so dumb. I thought my future
wife would be so proud I waited for her. kind of. you get my second virginity
this is my gift to you and the world such honor in sacrifice
it wasn't religious it was dumb
poor noell she wasn't having a relationship between finger blasts
and tender strokes she unlocked my want in a parking garage and
an el torito women's restroom.

I'm 27. the curly blonde waitress melissa with a gillette wit
from the potholder café in long beach
whom I was scared to talk to had a perfect
beach face and spaghetti hair and we broke

my bed and then she moved to the east coast
she would call me, fuck me hard with a fresh two apple ass
and little travel tits and leave me in devastation's bliss
there is medicine in us to share this can be good and fine
sometimes I wish she'd stayed in my life we both thought we would ruin it
by talking about what it was.
I am trying to say everything now

I'm 28 and I'm so poor and I didn't hit my goal checklist
and I didn't get married by 24 or find a house by 26
or take off as a writer by 28 but I'm still here and I feel good

I'm 30 and I finally stopped growing
courtney was short
she would come to my 300 dollar a month loft after the prospector
and let me go down on her while she was upside down,
midair, suspended in my arms like a dirty cirque du so what,
she would ask me to go up on her
her little legs stiffening to the ceiling when I'd find it
she wore booties with comics on them and the colors and the colors
she would scream so loud when she'd ride me,
I'd give bottles of wine to the neighbors the next day
this was the first time a woman seemed demon-possessed
while kissing me, full on loss of control
and she showed me how to get there
courtney's hair was curly seaweed and I loved it all over me
pure human lust, a woman I would dream about
her pussy tasted like a florist who masturbates a lot
she hated seeing cum on her and didn't tell me for a month
I wish we all talked more and not hope for the best
I told you I say everything now
I ask about everything now

THE CRIMINAL

Your beauty is a rhythm
I can't wait to forgive.

I want my teeth on your shoulder. Softly.

I want to perch on it and heal.

Milkshake-suck your lips down
until my heart becomes voltage and free energy.

And maybe, if there's time,
I want to live long off the turret of your neck.
A docile bite. The almost of it all.

Fall upon me godless.

The small sting of you wincing
close to me—
to tease a slow fang into your wrist.

A
hunt of softness
summoning.

Love.
If there's a little blood
I will smear and become it.

I will drink and taste,
mouth bones teasing for delicate capture—
turbinado sugar haul of your tattooed legs.

Let go in my spit
and I'll suck all the needled art from you—
turn my teeth black. Goodbye rockabilly cherries.

Curves of hip skin—thin with
the shiverbumps raising the hairs, bone-terrified of all
I'm holding back. A tender yes, yes.

In the morning
you will not leave,
but you will be gone.

They asked what I wanted
for my last meal.

All of you is fair.

Never tell a Night Thing
without days remaining
that he can have anything.

THE FLASHER AND THE SEA
for Terry Sitz

There are no fish scales
on the black cutting board

To her, they are stars stuck
to the flat matte plastic black sky

To her, the sea is a thing to talk to, a cobalt cloak
swinging open with a fringe of white like a cursed flasher

To her, every nervous princess
is just a Maltese from another lifetime

To her, pink
is now

Every vase
is a holder of temporary dazzles

There are no trees in the distance
but sentries waiting to come to life in the land of no names

To her, risk is something to trust
instead of trust being something to risk

It was in you since fifteen
the eyes behind the eyes

To close the breezing veils of what you were
and let the inner lasers do their work

To her, home is a pair of arms
that feel like some sophomore dance slow song that won't let go

How we marvel at the eye behind your eyes
The ones that cuffed some unexpected science lab partner

There she is, your love, your longest love, the conclusion of love
healing in the garden

She is at fault and faultless
a seeing kind of beauty

You love her easy
so you let her be

TROPICAL DEATH

for Shayne Benowitz

The next time someone in flip-flops,
battered in tropical death, comes up to you
at The Green Parrot bar in Key West,
all Hey, baby girl and tells you that you have nice eyes,
I hope they see you are a collection of almost deaths.

Glad you escaped the O.C.
No one should die in the tank top party of Huntington Beach.
No one should die in the aloof sorrow of Newport Beach,
a town that has as much spirit as a Croc sandal with flair charms.

Glad you survived Florida.
No one should have to die in the lonely, heated pools of Miami.
Can we ever really know the mysterious crime air of the South?
No one should die in that much airborne sweat.

I hope this dude at the Parrot Bar catches your gaze and sees
that you are from nowhere. You are a walking escape hatch.

Someone will see that you are from a place to sail away from,
a woman observing, always In Another Country,
a force constantly blossoming into a Dangerous Summer,
a woman who can see the lost things in the eyes of others
and is unafraid to capture it all with an old ass camera.

Tell the men to go home empty handed
and to love alone, and live in quiet resolve
as music about paradise and cheeseburgers
churns in the humid silk of night.

Show sunburnt men
how to let the feeling of being from nowhere sink in.
Show them how to let the eyes sparkle knowingly
from the pendant of
a wandering, heart that breaks daily from little wonder,
little horror collections,
which is the only way to see.
Which is a great way to scare off the soft ones.
the soft ones.

SMALL WINDOWS IN THE YOGA PANTS

I wish it was Crème Brûlée Monday or Smash in Public Day,
but it's Laundry Day on the road again.

The clock ticks
like it's trying to get a hair off its tongue.

I'm on a big fat Yamaha Super Ténéré 1200 motorcyle
talking into a little helmet microphone, yelling
back at the wind in my ears and the ceremony before me
of a road unwinding like a celluloid film reel.
It's wonderful air to haul ass in, and I'm
trying to record this feeling as it happens.

Harry Nilsson at the bottom of my lungs,
commercial jingles for grocery outlet,
the subconscious unraveling along the tarmac.
Don't think of what you miss.
Record how beautiful a life with no appointments is.

I am quiet for days, except when screaming into the recorder.
Screaming close to death at 85 mph along the Beartooth Highway.

It's Fall in Love Friday! Nope. It's Laundry Day. Settle down.

I put four quarters in the wall machine for fabric softener sheets.
The older woman smiles at me, folding with sensual deliberation.
In the other aisle, a woman runs her nails across her long legs, lazily
fingering her phone, exhaling tiny and scrolling.
What's everyone eating in this town? Sex ham?

I was about to tell you how Bozeman, Montana,
feels like a horny Christian yoga retreat.
Two yoga moms sit down next to me at
the Farmer's Daughters breakfast cafe.
They just got done working out
and they smell like orchid Bounce dryer sheets. Little sheer windows
into their athleisure, diamond shapes up their thighs.

I listen. I listen and sip.
They ask about my jacket, nervous that I am dirty and
don't want to be bothered.

It feels so good to speak to someone.
It's Kevlar. Its an armored jacket, in case I fall.
"Well, don't do that."
It's all I try to do.

It would sound like poetry, if it wasn't surrounded by nervous giggles.
I ask them about their day. They skip it.
"Your bike is beautiful."

I want to say, you're beautiful. And
your husband's a liar. Get your hair knotted and your neck sucked.
Who wants to get on the back and smell their way back to life
and ruin their marriage?
I have room for one.
We can get you some warm clothes at Cracker Barrel.
And the good hashbrowns.
I want your yoga tights against me. I like the windows into your skin.
I want to hug you goodbye at the airport and not say anything,
your fake duck lips double pouting to kiss me one last time.
But it will never be as good as our kiss
by the bison field near the Chief Joseph Highway
where the twelve-point elk came
and stared at you getting it from behind.

Thanks. I like the blue rims.

Those are nice rims you got. Wish we could go for a ride.
One at a time ladies. Have a good weekend.
You too.

Off I ride into the skyline of fleece and guns,
puffy vests and raised trucks,
abortion billboards and Skechers everything,
a Costco country I am learning to love
as steady as the engine noise between my legs,
and I keep trying to sing with my visor open
without eating a bumble bee, wondering what dirty ass
muse sent me the phrase Sex Ham
when I wasn't ready for it.

SOME SONGS

One night, in the Alamitos Bay
I took the gondola out alone.
Melted gummy Coke bottle sea.

Everyone I loved
who died
came up from the water like a Busby Berkely bit.

And I turned up the Bluetooth speaker.
And they partnered up
and they waltzed on the water.

It felt so good to see everyone.
A little twirl in the twilight. It hurt my heart so much.
Come with me and I'll play that song for you for a long time.

QUIET AS A BURN PILE

Father, my blood share. The days are tightening.
I am quiet at your backyard trash burn pile.
We are waist-deep in your late seventies.
At lunch, I tell you, *There's a crumb on your mouth, Pop.*
You don't care and it's quietly funny to both.

Can you feel it?
Nope. It wants to be there.

I tell you *I found a watch*
in the pile—in the burning mound.
You stare down at the waiting dirt
and ask me if I said I had found a witch.
Yes, Pop. I found a witch and it has this melted
metal band. A little handcuff.
You don't flinch or laugh.

I tell you about your former love and wife, my soft mom.
That Ma's eyesight won't let her drive at night anymore.
That she is considering moving close to my sister's kids.
She is considering the end and how it will look to grocery shop,
having been gutted by God. And you don't
see the world beyond TV and AC and McDonald's.

I want to tell you
I used to hate you.
I used to want to beat you
harder than you beat me, I worked out to get strong,
to beat you
for your wander, misplaced anger, and belt buckle thrash.
But I just take another load of trash to the burn pile
and swallow my young hurt before making your potato salad.

You say, Thank you, son. You got it right. Pickles.
Yes, I remembered the kind with pickles.

I want to tell you how my life is crumbling,
as we stand over the garbage of your life, the waste in your wake . . .
I hear crackles of fire and grackles above, witch bone cinders,
you almost touch my hand.

Father. Endless Father. Cursed, Endless Father.
I plead my case for the last time.
Let me return this season to the silence we love.

To go back home
and wash down the burnt smoke of dying California
in a miracle of zinfandel and forget myself.
To walk across the sea to someone
who can't hold my want.
To sit alone like you, re-strategizing the past,
raising the dead like a grudge.

You are frail now.
You used to tell me to do as I was told
or you'd beat the "why?" out of me.
Pain taught me to do as I was told. Tell me what to do with my sad.

You and I used to wear a uniform,
and being ready to kill
meant you were a good boy who listened.
I was an obedient Pentecost.
Medals shining over my heart
for how hard I could obey—
a steady march to my honorable death.

I watch your toil and secret horror before me. In your *I give up* clothes.
You have a few years left, solo in the sticks.
Buying four foods. Potato salad. Chicken. Beans. Pie.
Tinker with the weed wacker. Leave it. You won't
let me fix the mower or take
out the trash or touch anything.
I need my things, you say. I wish I was a TV.

See me in your work, Father.
I watch you just to be with you,
as if some lesson can be learned.
This year, I am without a lover again, like you.
You want to end this way. I don't. I can't.

This next time I learn to love—
I will fall in love slower
and stay, like you once promised to Ma,
but every promise is a dish looking for a wall
in your trembling hand. I can't make out exactly what you mutter:

lowerme / medirt / lonermeformiles / boystuff / toysinaburnpile / dicedpickles
/ turdofcow / cowardcufflinks / stinkofunused / usedupjunktrinkets/
mygoldmyallthatsleft / allmygoldjunk/ myburnmyburnmyburn

Teen me still see's you, steam coming from your mouth,
and I know the words I needed from you
froze in your throat. You clear
some crap from the garage and load it in the burn pile.
Wearing the slippers I gifted you. Ruining them.

Father. This terrible waiting.
I cannot ruin your last years
with the truth.

BENEFITS

My stepdad takes his time when he speaks, Navy guy, says,

"The VA called randomly and told us our options
for my burial

because I turned eighty.

They'll give me a headstone and a plot for free,
but no ceremony. One of you has to
fill out the flag application from va.gov
or ask the funeral director to do it.

Since we are both veterans...

...we get a free flag when we go."

I thought we'd get more. A gun salute? I said.

He said, "No. Might scare neighbors.
I don't think either of us will get that.
I thought maybe they could pay to hold some swords
over my grave or something."

I would want that too.

"No dice. If I want a real funeral it is $8,500 for a viewing in a church.
$5,000 if I do a simple graveside ceremony and a four-sider casket."

It's weird to think about the cost to die.
I think we earned the right
to have some guys hold swords over our caskets.
There's a website called swordsdirect.com. Is four swords good or should I
see what eight would cost or twelve?

"Four would be plenty. Maybe none is plenty."

SOMEONE NAMED A STAR CLUSTER LOZENGE
for Zac

In my stove pot are three halved oranges,
some clove and cinnamon,
and I wait for it to boil.

I think of my older sister. In Kentucky. In a long dress.
We used to not talk
because of Covid arguments
and God stuff.

I wish I could make my sister happy and be a Christian
like her. After a while, I felt like a mission and not
her brother. I told her to stop calling me just to convince me
of eternity reservations. I told her it felt like sales.

Now we talk recipes and her kids and how cold she gets.

She and Ma taught me the wintertime
smell-good trick of making a home smell like a home.

I got home and boiled cloves and oranges in the winter black,
and I miss the three of us growing up together.

When I imagine the end is close
all I want is to be closer to the ones
I love. To beat them in ping pong again.
Explore white chocolate theft together.
Rename the constellations after cocktails.
Pillow fight explosions.

Near the Little Dipper is a star called
Lozenge. We now have proof that astronomers drop acid.
I will call her and talk about that.

Here's some advice for anyone in the family cuffs:
Pick up the phone and call the endless puzzle of your family.
Go easy on Roman history and Revelation
and listen to the thing in the breath
that is behind the "Oh hey—"
"What's up..."

Feel something lifting
like a heartbreaking smell,
a heartbreaking smell you love
that isn't interested
in selling a thing.

YOU ALMOST DIED
for Amber Tamblyn

No one should be alone with Jell-o.
I almost died, and Amber raced me to the hospital.

I can't see the high hospital wall TV.
Smells like nothing good visited this room.
One nurse wears some kind of teenage green apple perfume.
I want to plant her.

The drugs make me reimagine the Munich love affair with
the formerly childless Caro long ago. Broken bottle nights.
The drugs make me think Amanda is happy back in Nashville,
and all is well. Roaring down the backroads of Lieper's Fork.

I feel like strong horses came to my track and they all lost.
I just want something in this room to explode
and forge me an exit and someone sneak me out.
It's so ugly in here, I'd try and die too.
Hospitals should be the new galleries.

My mother shows up, tells me that I almost died,
asks me if my heart is right.

I do not know how to answer and tell her to check my EKG.
I don't know what's wrong with me.

She restates: I mean, I am wondering if your heart is right with the LORD.
You almost died. You still could die.
Don't you want to know where you'll spend eternity?

She is water-cooler-face pale, a thick San Francisco sadness.

If this is death's doorstep, it is boring.
No my heart isn't right. No I don't want to know about mansions in the air.

I only say the word, "Yes,"
and it makes her stop crying.

I just wanted her to stop crying.

MODERN FUZZ

When she calls,
her breath is cinched
and she cannot speak. You say,

"Babe? You there? What is it? Honey? Are you okay, Babe? Hello?"

She is holding her breath through the sparklers of pain
and tells you she has been bitten by a snake
while walking the dog.
She is swelling-green.
The ambulance can't get to the cabin
for almost an hour.

"I'm coming now . . . Babe. Hold on."

You race through the black silk
of two a.m. that conceals the world—
streetlights bend at you
like people trying to hand you water at a marathon.
Your eyes glow like sirens in the rearview mirror.
Not like.
It is police sirens in the mirror.

What's the hurry, son?

"Please! My . . . other . . . has been bitten by a snake!"

Your dog? Your twin?

"No sir. My person. My total babe."

A legal guardian or chaperone?

"No sir. My boo. My lady partner."

Your wife?

"No. Not wife. Please, sir. She may be bleeding out. She's not my wife. She is my.
. . one."

Oh. Just say your girlfriend and don't be all suspicious.

"Not trying to be suspicious sir. But she thinks 'girlfriend' is infantilizing."

But you call her babe, which is probably the ultimate in infantilizing.

"We all make deals with the devil. But no to girlfriend, and definitely not just my girl. More than a friend. My specialness."

A lover?

"We feel lover suggests a kind of purely sexual ownership and feels anti-intellectual. We settled on 'respected substantial connection' for a year, but it was a bit stiff to say during intimacy. But please, can you escort me? My noteworthy and meaningful accomplice is bleeding to death!"

This a long-term relationship?

"We feel that long-term is subjective. Barely three years. We don't want to feel the pressure of a label."

What in the hell do you call her when you introduce her?

"I just say her name. I introduce her as her name."

Like a co-worker.

"No. Please, my . . . forever person . . . could be dying!"

Ironic to have a forever person die. Are you in love with this forever person?

"We are compatible and we are successfully cohabitating. So I love. . . that."

I'm going to need you to step out of the car.
You're hiding something, son.
If my wife, whom I often hate
but am connected to by the blurry and cable-like synapses of love,
if my wife, whose eyes were born in the hands of some *midnight jeweler,
if she was dying, I would not have stopped. I could not have stopped.
So. You have the right to remain silent.
Silent as a winter lake that calls to your warm blood.
Silent as God's answers.
Silent as dead love at the breakfast table.

Anything you say can and will be used against you
in an illogical laundry room spat.
Logic puts love in the ground.
Love is an insane declaration of dependence.
It wants to see you bleed in its terrifying spotlight.
You have a right to hear you are loved and to be owned by love.
Do you understand the rights I have just read to you?

"But it's so scary."

This whole thing is scary and scary is good. Now let go rescue
your co-habitating allyship. She seems like a total boo-boo.

"Oh. We're not at boo-boo yet."

CHAPTER WHERE THE AUTHOR MURDERS THE MIDNIGHT JEWELER

BREEZE ADMISSION

I am afraid there is no one left

I am afraid that what I had was as good as it gets

I am afraid no one will want me that way again

I am afraid I'll be haunted by her perfect orgasm cosmology

I'm afraid she doesn't miss my cock or oaky kiss or hazel-hazel

I'm afraid I'll never taste her body again, the deep broth
and chipped citrus

I'm afraid I will never want to stop sucking all her down feathers
into the blankets of my body

I am afraid she got bored

no

that I expired

I am afraid she'll get excited about the newness
of stronger hands and cool city smilers

I am afraid she won't dream about the adventures we planned
as hard as I still do

I am afraid there's not enough in here

I am afraid that I will see her tangy smile when declaring devotion to a new
medicine cabinet

I am afraid I still want to record her sound
hands across skin sound
her suffering dead moan sound
when I rub her shoulders deep sea sound

I am afraid no one will want my outdated song

I am afraid that it feels normal without me
too fast, too easy to shed
This is how living is for a body covered in antennaes

I am learning to reconcile the fact
that it isn't hard for anyone to be without me

Why did I agree to meet

I am afraid she can tell I jerked off to a video
of her laughing, about an hour before we have coffee to talk about
how great we both are doing

I'm afraid I'll go back to praying as the loneliness gets so bright

I'm afraid I'm looking for something invisible to lean on
which always gives way

I am tired of looking for a love that is the full force of the hurricane

Some people live good with just a little breeze
to keep them cool in the heat
They seem at ease, fearless,
like the love they have is easy as looking at a mountain
without having to climb it
to enjoy it

THE FIRST KISS AS THE LAST KISS

The first kiss was heavy-heavy
and the last kiss was murder

The last kiss was too much teeth
and wondering when to run
to the deep snow and dive
to cool the heat

The last kiss, it ended me
and the last kiss was hunger
for another last kiss
that was less of a gold hardening in the throat
and less wanting air
and new jewelry

The last kiss was known to be
the last kiss by the other party
The last kiss was brutal and soft
like the slobber of shore break

The last kiss is always on a couch
you can never lay on again

PHLOX

The summer of wallow too hard.
The summer of finched color.
Sidewalk drunks assassinated my birds
of paradise. We could still be together.

I deserve every morsel of paranoia.
The night is still hunting me.
Does this jacket make me look like an exit?
We could still have the child.

You summoned me
like I could skip the line at the fair
for watermelon summer.
We could be one admission apart.

You reached into the rind with a lead fist
and pulled out the center,
and my heart stopped.
We could have better lives.

You crammed it in my mouth, and my heart
beat again. Magical animal.
We could resurrect the sails of desire.

Pulp gulp. Grandeur
dripping down my face like a teen pink sunset.
Your godless face, your gift to my puzzle.
We could be in pillows.

My tears flow
for some dog
to come and taste.
We could try and try after trying.

You forgive me, and Death Valley
is blown from every map.
We could wander and end.

You forgave me.
Arms full of phlox,
and I vomited monarchs.
We both hear children scream in the park,
not sure if it's joy.

We could be us
if surrender
was on the table.

HUNGER SLING

In the dumbest year of the heaviest light
I worshipped nutmeg tea and staring.

I bowed down to television light.

I pressed my skin against the sunflower
wallpaper and prayed for arms to emerge.

The year of nothing is real anymore. Time erased. Saviors gone deaf.

The year of nothing is all I want to feel.

I was hungry at last.

The Danes call it *hudsult* or skin hunger.
The Dutch called it *huidhonger*, the want for contact.

I miss people I haven't met.
I love and long for people who once loved me—
the bad ones.

The French brought me *confinema*—
the jamming of confinement and cinema
when you are alone in a TV spree, becoming couchness.

I love the music of the Spanish potion: *cuaranpena*—
the marriage of quarantine
and sorrow.

                    ★

Every hug, a noble risk.
I see them in the park.
I feel my skin nodding and reaching.

The following image will be
the next thing
you dream about.

Remove all the clothes from the closet and
lean into the coat hanger bones. What a crowd.

Paying someone to touch me and look under the hood
doesn't seem so kinky anymore—
it doesn't seem so scary to ask.
Every dog shall be hugged without request.

I've had some touch.
How the JoJo's burger girl's handful
of change felt like fresh
air without a mask.

★

I hold the pounds now.
I miss a theater of strange ones—I miss everyone's skin.
Shouting from a pulpit: *I'm not good at this.*

How long the year of dancing alone and steady sobbing.
Unbuckling your belt and crying at the mess,
maybe I'm being taught
how to remember what a Tic Tac is for.

My lonely dance reveals loaves of grief, a rusted
lust, an inherent magical sadness,
My beautiful, field-wide sadness.

Call all your friends, dying in the same way as you.
Thank your beloved pillow, the pretender, for being there.

Here's to making it this far
and toasting the chosen
who didn't sneak out from under the evil invisible
and had to soar early.

Here's to settling in the present couchness and being grateful,
soaked in orange turmeric stains,
learning to caress the walls and kiss the windows,
my heart and its ability to blank onstage,
my very real skin hunger rising,
begging this nutmeg tea
to taste like the chapstick of someone
born to come and save me.

MISCOUNTED BULLETS

And tonight, it covers me:
I may not pull off these dreams.
I may not make it to old age,
may have to vacate the premises.

Ran out of light too fast,
I loved out,
like miscounting bullets
in the barrel.

The white dress was too heavy
to carry,
the guest list
too long to afford.

I never wished
my life would end up
this weird
and empty at night.

Stroll and smell
everyone
making dinner.
What courage to knock and say I'm starving.

What am I here for?
Who am I for ?
Who was I ever
for?

This
is a book
called
How to End a Book When You're Sick of Writing It.

Whatever I'm meant to learn
from the coiling
from this slow destroy
I don't like it, lowercase lord.

The difference in the eyes
of wanting something and being forever haunted by that wanting
is so big.
It's too big—

and the thunder comes and
brings
me
perfume.

ACCIDENTAL SUICIDE

The house was drowning me.

My house was filled with love and linens.
A rainy world kept us indoors most of the time.
Our shoes next to each other by the door,
pine needles stuck to the wet edges.
A pie on the kitchen counter in a pink box
for dinner that night.
It can't officially be called our last pie
because it was thrown away three days later. After you tired.
Trash pie.
Thrown away when I moved out.

I didn't want to move out. I didn't want to feel ugly.
I didn't want it to end, even when I wasn't wanted.
I dream of drainage ditches filling.
I won't ever dream in this house again.
Photos in frames of places I can't ever go with anyone else.
It's like a dog pissed all over Spain and Vegas, Normandie,
Hat Yai, and Nangs.
Trash those too.

A tree in our yard fought the breeze that day, tapped the glass, wanted to load its
arms through the window as the wind poltergeisted. O life in a hazard of rain. O
life somewhere else. O systems of surprise, how you sneak up on me.

It was raining that morning, sad cartoon. Of course.
My house smelled like coconut cream. Once.
My house forgot how to summer.
My house forgot how to fuck.
My house forgot how to go easy on each other.
My house had a tool shed, and I cleaned it and never got a chance
to build anything.
It's all yours. It's your house. It's your dog now.
My home flooded in gray, and it fits you
like a catsuit, and I hope you know I don't own anything. Your body.
I wanted into your body. Dreamt, I finally got in like a shrunken
Dennis Quaid in *Innerspace*.
Inside I began to drown in all that water, and all I wanted was out
when I finally got in.
How do you not get drunk and call me slurring as a consolation prize?

First, you like being small in their veins, then you can't breathe when the blood thins, and you either die from smallness or get passed through the intestines into the light.

I have been shit out.

This house is flooding as I move my stuff into a U-Haul. I accidentally said I never want to talk to you again.

I couldn't figure out the money. If I could've figured out the money, I would have been a future most wanted. I could have looked like a home. I know there is a home in me.

Empty as Dad's wallet. If I could have figured out the money,
I could have saved so much . . .
my uncle Gene's leg.

My dad said Gene committed accidental suicide. He wanted some car insurance money and tried to crash in a ditch, it snuck up on him fast—he braked, but his bum leg must have freaked, accelerated too much, and flipped the slight pickup, and a married man drowned alone at night in Texas. I know how badly he wanted out, hand against the glass window, as if he was ever strong enough to escape, realizing his plan wasn't his plan, but someone else watching from the treetops.

I can't die in the ditch.

I ordered coconut cake today at lunch. It had lemon in it,
and my eyes opened wide when I bit in
as if I had never had it before.

METAMORPHOSIS

The lobster hisses when dropped in the pot—
the snake in its heart, vanishing from its carapace.

I loved walking around the lagoon with you after fancy dinner.
The goopy marshland water blended into the night sky,
lost its identity and looks like one big rampart with ducks climbing up
the shimmering black wall of starlight.

I can't go back to losing myself inside you.
You were loyal to your parents' sadness.
I didn't try hard enough to understand.

I hold your laugh inside me
like a metal pacemaker
and am worried about security.

Your face would Christmas tree
when I would see you at the airport.
I miss being doused in you.

I wound a lever and crushed a penny in the machine
to get a souvenir,
to remember my day alone at Knott's Berry farm.

It cost 50 cents to ruin the penny, 51 cents.
It wasn't a good deal. What am I going to do with it?
Learn something?

I'm not sure what a relationship costs.
Things are learned. Things are unlearned.

I like summoning the good times.
Lagoon times. The pond as a wall we could walk into and swim to the moon.

I long for the truce to end the war
with my instinct
to shred all documents.

IN SWEATS, IN DEATH

The sweatpants ended us.

Strange, you want to get closer to your lover,
and if you get too close for too long, you pass through them.

We stuffed the fuzzy cuffs of sex and desire
in a bag and threw it in the lake to rust—

the dead lake between us
somehow got deader.

At night, the hopeless bed reminds me
I used to be a person that was held.

Memory foam is the worst gift
for heartache.

I used to be soothed by light snoring.
I used to make the one with fangs laugh so hard,
her teeth would get snagged in the ceiling.

I used to love someone that would fuck me
with their eyes open
for two of the four years.

I felt her eyes turn away from me nightly
into some handsome world.
She said, "I'm just not attracted to you anymore,"
handed me a robe for the diving contest
into the ugly well.
I swam slowly in my happy fat, and now
I work out all the time,
hoping to fuck someone silly who has memorized
the way out, someone who doesn't like their cocktails sweet.

It's not working.

The pawnshop rejected the engagement ring,
said it was too unique—too hard
to melt down and find any value in.

So off into the Willamette you soar.
In the air, the ring sheds its memories
like cicada carcasses.
The cliffside proposal, the Sunday roast, the first time on skis—
they floated there in a pink mist
as the ring slipped
from its skin,
plunked—

        O

           O

               O

and then those white gold, tiny diamond
and Honduran wood memories
wheezed into nothing.

In my sweats, I bake sweet potatoes
until they are black
and sweet enough
for me.

RABBIT HOLE

We do weird things when we are sullen turds.

I have watched five versions of U2's "With or Without You" on YouTube
and I stopped listening to them in High School
and I never want to feel High School again and I am so confused and pregnant
and when he sings it in Milan on the second night
Bono is tired and he is as frazzled as a grunge sweater like
when my nerves are shot and all light has left the portholes of my hull
and it's the rare night when it hurts
that no one waits for me to come home
and it's fine
and you feel like a cave that collapsed and the miners inside want to live
but the news cycle has moved on
and when he sings this time he asks the audience to help him sing
cause his voice is shot
and I want this song to be over because U2 was
for my teenage desperation and I have moved on
and I hate U2 now
but I am feeling something from the song again and OH NO
I have shit to do
and the song is so wrong
I *can* live with or without you
but one is more fun.

And Bono is too tired to go on singing
waving the mic into the wet night sky high above the audience . . .

Wait. There it is. I see the thing inside his body
that begs him to go for the last big note
and he does and empties the tank and
Haaaa-ahhh-oooooooh!
I'm sixteen and singing out my melted guts with him
until the neighbor
bangs on my wall, says, *Hey! You nailed it!*

I say, You damn right I did. Say it again!

He yells, "*Last time I'm gonna say this. Shut the fuck up.*"

THE GRIP LOOSENS

chopsticks/ no fun/ for a/ nervous man
     people fill the rodeo grounds/ the gore option awaits
          I have plenty of time to make it/ reduced to pratfalls

here it come/ here it always almost come
     the bull is mad/ Velcro belt around his gut
          we are currently not booking at this time/ beg for slots

it's slipping from my sticks!
     the bull/ no longer confused/ blood hungry revenge snort
          no one's in the mood for you/ dying onstage nightly

my grip/ loosening/ looser than drunk shakes on a chopstick grip
     no one cheers for the bull/ when it wins
          modern times/ moved on from me/ is all spunk and fear posing

poke the soft carrot/ it breaks apart too/ I still can't ask for a fork
     cowboy up when trampled/ the rescue clown is bleeding
          run the light/ how much time do I have left?/ dead silence

I want to eat so badly/ my whole life is wet noodles/ trembling hands
     hold on for eight seconds/ this life
          Someone hold me or laugh at my jokes/ same thing

A beautiful young couple
     waiting/ patient
          for my sloppy table/ but this is mine/ until I or the heavens call it

CROOKED CONSTELLATIONS

I am quiet in the insomnia apartment.
I feel a lead hand shove my chest,
reduce me down to the kitchen floor.

Too many of my single friends my age
died of heart failure, last short breaths on the floor—
last thing seen, crumbs—
and they didn't have weak hearts,
they had big hearts—too big
and they didn't have the money to fix it
and burst from empathy and want.

All the constellations
are her crooked body sleeping
when I am alone.

Something was mounted to her.
I couldn't unsaddle it.

The world isn't set up to be single.
I didn't want to be single.

I see the mirror disassembling me.
I look like someone who will start the diet
tomorrow
again.

I stay in it longer than I should.
I am waterlogged and pruney
near the end. Loved 'forever' too much.

Forever is an orphan:
a word you once were excited to adopt,
but because of its boorish behavior,
it is a word you no longer wish
or need to see
or owe anything to at all.

When I look
at the car we bought with the bad emergency brake,
it is so sad.

It is too big of a car
and begs me
to sell it to a family, clumsy with the Cheerios.

I am alone, and you are in love again
and there is no more talk of fairness,
and I have burned through so much
mouthwash trying to relearn
the human Autotrader of online dating.

No one has time for a new story.

Two a.m. is too cold to smile,
too quiet to unbrass the dawn with singing,
so it sounds like someone is with you.

Don't wear these clothes to bed again.
Go stretch.
Go eat.
Remember you are bad at stocking the fridge.

The grocery is open late. Would be good to see a person.
At Perfect Foods Market
there is a howl in the meat department, "Make it quick, Steve!"
and a sign above says fresher than fresh. All willing meat.

Carton of eggs! Sale! One dollar!
What a deal.
Someone has partitioned them into 2 per little carton, for that single life!

Three-month supply of toilet paper!
It's just two rolls.
Oh.

Everything is slimming down around me.
The big box store was busier. "I want to sample and frump!"
Families buy in bulk and frump cozy all day..

The dessert section here is empty.
The tissue section is empty.
The wine aisle is empty.

The diaper aisle is stocked full.
The flower department is bored.
The words family-size have been censored from every package.

The lights inside are dim.
The floors are slippery.
No flirting after one p.m.

Of course
it's always been emotional
self-checkout.

It feels like an art installation,
the wall of alcohol, little airline bottles,
buy one, get five hundred free and build
some sort of fortress for dum-dums.

I am home.
I am keeping some dumplings in the bag.
Being single is leftovers, is a memory of a good meal and enduring it again.

I always just want one glass of wine,
but it always tastes like shit a day or two later
and corking it feels like I gave up,
so I just drink it all.
Tonight I'll eat all the dumplings.
I am so sick
of reliving everything.

DRUNK TEXTS TO THE HEAVENS

DESIRE IS A CANTEEN I CANNOT FILL

MY MADNESS IS WONDER ADDICTION

I LOSE YOU IN THE MAZES OF A BETTER LIFE

I LOSE YOU IN THE WIDE ARMS OF SOMEONE ELSE'S MUSIC

I TURN MY CHIN TO YOUR GHOST HAND
AND SUCK IT DOWN MY THROAT
LIKE A FOG-THICK NIGHTSTICK

MY FACE AS RED AS WET BEETS AND WARMING

ALL THIS GOES INTO THE AIR BEFORE IT GETS TO YOU

CALL ME WHEN SMASHED AND WANTING

YOU MEMORIZED MY NUMBER

THAT'S HUGE

I MEAN I'M SAYING I'M HERE

I MEAN I'M SAYING I KNOW PEOPLE CHANGE

I MEAN I STILL MEAN WHAT I USED TO MEAN

YO, YOU UP?

WHY MANY AUTHORS LOVE ACID

Too many authors love acid,
and I can't tell if they are writing
or if the acid is writing its way to stardom
off the blubbering host.

Maybe we can say that about writers in the throes of
grand staircase heartache.

It's a drag when writers can't see beyond themselves.
I also don't like it when waiters do a little laugh
when I say don't want dessert.

I miss talking about the night, the sky as a place to end up.
I miss the smog sometimes. It's a better sunset.
It's a sunset we participated in.

HOW TO BE RIGHT ALL THE TIME

Can you please try New Orleans again with me?
Wander off all you want.

Can you wait and see if I strike gold in Los Angeles?
I'll get skinnier.

Can we end the argument in Nashville that never ends?
I'll be softer and give you those kids.

Can we redo Indiana and hold your mother until she sleeps?
I'll let her win. I'll pretend she didn't kiss me.

Can Texas be a place we look forward to being in a storm together?
I will stop wishing for new homelands.

I know I am just visiting this body.
It yearns for an end.

I thought I'd know so many for a long time.
I forget that a text can be a guillotine.

"I thought you'd like this book."
"Thanks. Great cover. How's your life."
"Good as can be."

"I'm good. How's the fam?"
"So good. Same old, same old."

NO! NO! NO! WE WEREN'T READY!
WE WOULD HAVE LASTED
IF WE STARTED SOME OTHER YEAR!
I'M READY FOR THERAPY!

"Whatchu up to?"

TRYING TO REMEMBER I ONCE WROTE
I DON'T NEED FIREWORKS
TO THINK THE SKY IS BEAUTIFUL!

"I mean, I'm good."

LET ME ADMIT I'M WRONG
IN PORTUGUESE, IN TONGUES,
IN ANYTHING.

"You loved being right."

It loved me first.

I ALSO HATE SEEING A BABY
IN A LEATHER MINI SKIRT

big sur steams
plaskett beach is a weird place to be alone
because it's so pretty
and there's no one to tell

I ride the licorice curves
kids climb dead trees
turkey vultures hulk over the flattened skunk

light a fire
think of the time when I traded love for peace

justin townes earle is singing for memphis mornings
into the camplight
and I am a kind of silence
and silences are broken
and a southern heart is heavy
and everyone can see me blown apart

one beer exploded the good one
down to one cheapo left
i don't want to drown in any river
don't even want to know why it sounds
so romantic to me this year

sit in the warm sand
singing *don't give up please don't give up*
at the top of my lungs
the gulls are scared of me and should be
I am bloated on the serene
time to start the new year's list of awful feelings
and
figure out where I can burn it

the night is a train that breaks down
the night is a skeleton wishing for the skin of daylight
the night is a baby with a sparkler in a leather skirt

i am cold under my clothes
under the embering light of morning
wishing there were lips to kiss
or puffed rice cakes to kiss
i have this morning forever now as
the music of dead men
call from the speakers
reminding you
to respect
where you're at

its fine that it hurts
at least I can feel another ocean
for a little while

A MERCY MOST NATURAL

The desert apologizes for all the killing.
There's little comfort, little mercy in the wilderness.
Mercy is not natural.

Stop under
an overpass
as it rains.

The air is clean as warm sheets until
the high desert rains come and tease the dying
Badlands with creosote and thin mud, ground steaming.

I step into the rain.
A momentary break
from the suffering light above.

I walk into the applause of tiny drops in puddles as the storm dies.
Damp air of sage blooms
broadcasted tumbleweed.

I go from soaked
to bone-cinnamon dry
in minutes.

I assign myself to this world.
I need to stay.
I forget why I need to stay.

All my sorrow a desert,
all the campsites I can afford, booked.
I put a Motel on a credit card and cry.

Pepsi and Funyuns.
I hate Pepsi.
I hate not having money.

I don't cry, I soft rain. I rain often,
common as a night stroll in the groomed burbs.
I rain to scare the desert inside, to hold it from expanding.

I'm dying in a nation of broken trampolines.
Knowing where you are is different
than knowing where you're supposed to be.

I feel it all when I am alone in a motel.
Polyester comforter air.
Blacklight nightmare.

Writing all this feels like I am wrapping a coat tie around my neck,
fastening it to the doorknob
and wondering if I'll cum or suffocate.

I wish someone was here to annoy me.
I wish someone would steal the comforter.
I wish my bed vibrated.

On a family trip, I'm so small. My parents got an earthquake bed
at a motel 6 and you put eight quarters in
and the headboard was mounted to the wall,
so we couldn't get to the plug to turn it off.

It shook all night long like the world's
saddest AC/DC ballad.
My mother slept next to me on the floor. That was so good.

Dry lightning is an eerie thing falling from heaven. Sudden thud.
When I want a traffic light to change I say ". . . aaaaand now!"
Pretending I can call the flash down, I yell "aaaaand, now!"

Timed it right once and killed
a shy lobby of groomsmen.
Love is too short for shy.

It appears my job is dreaming
of you, and I have been drinking
on the job.

I was mad.
I stayed—
I am the one who stayed. No one else to be mad at.

I smell the soft bonfire chemicals
of someone smoking in the parking lot.
My father's brand.

I lean on the rail. A voice from below says, "Hey, can I come up?"/
"Who are you?" I say. /
"An anvil. An anchor. A fridge full of foods that will make you unfuckable." /
"Come on up."/

Maybe I won't be in this hotel, on this road long.
Maybe I will sprain my ankles, whiskey tango solo on rotted dance floors
and enjoy my last alone.

When you tango alone,
you look like an idiot.
You look like a widow without a shadow.

You look like you can't let go
of a prom ghost who is politely passing the time with you
while waiting for their lover to come back from the bathroom.

I try but can't let go of a hope that I will find a prom crasher,
a flamenco turmoil, a tempest of storm-twisted flowers
who whispers in my ear, boy, boy full of useless rain.

I have come
to erase your grave.

DIRTY / NO DIRTY

You don't roll around in the wet sand
under rock-hard moonlight
under a low-tide dock

You don't kiss anyone
whose tongue is a swinging gate into their mind
whose lips are avocado ripe and
and whose breasts heave with cold want

You don't know anyone
who asks to be fucked
then asks for it slower
and can say what they need
and are okay with cumming loud
enough to spark the wheels of the chariot into fire
for the end of days

You don't voodoo
You don't sing and float
You don't die right
You don't cool enough

She likes musicals and upbeat cat porn
You are heavy with visions of the moon exploding
from exhaustion
You smoked all your guardian angels and
coughed them as clouds of trouble

You don't have anyone to doze off with
To taste and oil up
To be outstretched upon and wailing silent
No one to hand a biscuit to

You don't know anyone whose hands
feel like kerosene born to ignite your lighthouse
A slow run up the thigh's power plant
You don't know people who satisfy

You don't hear the waves while sneaking a mack-sesh
when everyone is asleep

You don't feel your shoes sinking
into wet sand as she begs for more
Her glad tits and fingers pressing into the collapse of beach below
going deeper and deeper still

Except for tonight
Four horsemen break from the sky
a welcome cry bellows
The kiss is locked
She is a siren in a crystal bodice
She is the harbor thirsting for more storm
She is the horizon pressing out the last light of day
The body needs and is unashamed at last
Even tomorrow comes fast

You could be this soaked and filthy and perfect
all the time
You could be anything if you would leave the house more
and shake the magic eight ball in your throat
until it says "Yes King Yes"

MURDER OF THE MIDNIGHT JEWELER

When I am in love
I try and make the stars
more than they need to be.

I try to say they are
the work
of some loving midnight jeweler.

Drilling, welding, and setting stones
in the long, glooming, achromatic bands above.

And it's a bit much.

I am tired of miracling everything.
It's a fridge, not a glacial coffin of nutrients.
They're stars. Not a glitter implosion of wonder.
They don't care. God has a kink in her neck
and can't look down anymore.
Why should I keep looking up for answers?

When I am lonely, there are fewer stars
and less sidewalk whistling,
and I hear the plants screaming for daylight
and the birds begging for help
instead of songing.
I don't belong in the logical world.
I want to be the midnight jeweler again.

But it seems like the moon just orbits and orbits around the earth
and can't just move on. Is it a sign of longing?

What if it's a tipsy moon each night,
intently listening, windows open
as the humming earth does the dishes?

Like the moon, I have a job to do—
to magnet around love like a compass needle, yearning, wanting,
lusty as a boy with a cantaloupe warmed in the microwave.

I want to be the midnight jeweler again.

Where my job is to make out in under-heated hot tubs,
to get hexed by wealthy warlocks and gun nuts,
to have shitty writers want to kill me,
and to have lovers draw my shape in the sand until
the tide comes to do what it does best to the shore.

Before the murder of the midnight jeweler,
I was
animated dust.
A chatterbox to strangers.
A force that renamed things.
I saw things no one saw.
I was a full magic trunk.
An odd camera.
The mood ring of Athena and Lenny Bruce.

When I am lonely, the supernatural
is just natural.

When I am lonely,
my phone is pretend-broken, just an ear warmer.
A scrollable photo album of half-truths.

When I am lonely, I don't remember
what I have.

I keep orbiting around the last good thing.
All my assets turn invisible in lonely light.

I need to be burnt and freed into the air
like a paper lantern, released with the best of intentions
of releasing a wish
but remembered for catching a breeze, igniting the bag,
falling fast, streaking the black sky in fire,
scorching a little league field
as a cold wash of stars
hovers blindly above.

CHAPTER WHERE THE AUTHOR GOES ALL IN AND PUTS HIS LAST FUCK TO GIVE IN THE JUKEBOX OF JOY

VISION BOARD

I have something scary to tell you:

In Mt. Carroll, Illinois,
Jim and his wife set up the Raven's Grin Inn,
a five-story former hotel that since the '80s has been converted
into a come-when-you-want haunted house.

They live in it.
If Jim is in a good mood,
the tour can last three hours.

There is a cat named Mr. Tuxedo,
a six-foot skull mounted to the house,
slides that vanish down into secret passageways
and a New York taxicab mounted like it crashed into the front door
permanently.

You can rent the whole thing and play hide-and-seek.
They love each other.

I don't want to die in an office.
I want to find someone who yells *Yahtzee!*
when they cum.
Take me to a weird beach in San Pedro and sleep on me warming.
A love life that is one long courtesy flush.
A partner who never asks which Aloha I mean.

Goof-whistler in the garden of serious men.
Take me to a hot spring and ruin me. Boil my sorrow
and rust me out
with your half-smile.

Fill the watermelon with vodka and take it
to the party and don't tell anyone. Not even the kids.
Throw their iPads in the fire and say it's a sacrifice to the digital gods.
Microdose with me under the Christmas lights.
I want days with you that are easier than pancakes.

Friendlier than a Canadian who grew tired
of being labeled as just friendly but
then went through a really hard time and leaned on their friends
and made a conscious choice to take a poll and the winning vote was
to get hella friendly again.

Pornstar courage in your heart.

Trying like a melody
that needs to be remembered.

I'll be a good business.
I'd love some company.

I want to build something
very, very
scary with you.

TIGHT SECURITY AT THE ETERNAL HOTEL

for Maggie and Scott

I pull the late shift doing security at the Eternal Hotel.
Keys on my hip jangle like a broken tambourine.

Check the doors. Check the gates. Make sure no one
steps into forever
drunk drowning in the infinity pool.

Make sure no one smashes the honeymooners' car windows
and takes the blenders, the espresso machines, the crock pots.

I always wonder how many people actually carry their bride
over the threshold of this spooky hotel.

It's just a strip of wood
holding the line between two worlds.

I never thought about the metaphor of transporting someone
from one world into the other until now.

Until I watch
the hallway security monitor.

In one room of the hotel, a homeschooled girl
wears so much purple electric neon.

She sings "The Time Warp" at the top of her lungs
until the ceiling bursts into a zodiac show of starlight.
No one complains.

In conference room Eden, the chandeliers come alive at midnight
slow waltzing until dervishing, a blur of warm beam.

In the lobby, a leggings model writes a novel about fairies
that come to lift her glass mother back to the ballet when she sleeps.

In the pool's locker room,
a father is softened by cigar smoke.

He teaches his sons about *Apocalypse Now* and punches a mirror,
swears they will not follow the troubled guides he once swore allegiance to.

From the back of the mirror,
a specter releases and creeps off into the jungle outside.

One couple takes turns carrying each other
over the door jamb, lifting
and struggling beautiful, the weathered luggage
a willing submission.

They stop laughing. They hold each other's faces, lost in a heft of wonder,
and it begins to rain red from the fire sprinklers.

They drink it in. I let it rain.
I let it flood the hall. Happens all the time.

I watch these two forces, weightless in blood-colored funk,
swimming with their lover,
crossing from one world into the other.

WEIGHTED BLANKET

for Jason and Jordy

Most people don't tell their kids
that much of life is goodnight dreams.
Goodnight, far away friends.
Goodnight, former soft ones.

We don't reveal to kids how some danger is fun
and whiskey hurts, and you need it to hurt,
and loneliness makes you stupid.
Goodnight, good choices.

We have a hard time telling kids
the wheels slip off. For every kiss
remembered, there are a dozen pictures of lovers
tossed in the burn pile. You wish them well.
Goodnight, ninety-nine-cent romance novels.

We wish we knew more truths earlier to ease this life.
We aren't trained how to fight right
without swinging wild and breaking our own jaws.
Goodnight to hopes of leaving
this world scarless.

We settle into the weighted blankets of night.

We aren't sure how to handle it
when the love of your life shows up, a suffering comrade
sitting across from you, agreeing that dry crepes
are the end of our species.

We aren't sure how to imagine the future
the first night you smell her brain, her beautiful circuitry
audacious in front of you, ready to destroy the love you knew,
smelling like a night sky full of Hawaiian pikake, and you are buzzed on it.
Goodnight solo laundry day.
It's nice to be haunted.
When she is gone, she is still there.

You begin to learn the codes in each other's little lighthouses,
she falls for your caramel fading twang.
You fall for her gentle want at the bar,

a queen hiding her crown under miles of curls,
still bouncing in the dim light of Ye Rustic Inn,
still not knowing it's a date until you offer to pay,
wing sauce on your Kenny Rogers Roasters face.
You're done. She holds you. You're done.
Now, there's music when there's no music.

In the dawn, a song to sing to the kids, a new warning:

Good morning my stumbling and bruised ice skate denier.
No one knows how to do this! Many know how to do this!
Good morning my inferno carousel.
Good morning my pile of Peeps destroyed in the microwave when we were high.
Good morning my tennis swing screamer.
Good morning my High Plains snow light.
Good morning my low tide, swamped-up porch song.
Good morning my shower jukebox and bad joke librarian.
Good morning my positivity forklift, lifting me from a sea
of boundless anxiety
into the rickety porno treehouse fortress
of your crumbling body.

Good morning.
The world is fading around us.
Good morning anyways, endlessy, my dear.
You will live in me, unburied.
Good morning, again and again,
until the wheels fall off.

DO YOU BLAZE?

I don't care
if a fire truck shows up
and it's dirty.

There they are, handsome servants
endlessly
washing and polishing.

I think we forget
what a thing is for
and how it's supposed to get, naturally.

I am fine
if you
show up dirty
to save me.

RUN IT OUT

I wish I was in the Oregon river water with you,
mint and cold when the forest smelled
like a rearview mirror air freshener
and the afternoon sky
looked like smoked cotton candy.

I wish for those dark mornings,
when the headlights of dawn shined through our window and
I made loose tea, and you woke and held me and introduced yourself,
and I couldn't wait for the sunlight to warm on in
to cook me slightly out of the frost.

I wish I could buy all twenty of your baby teeth.
The first hard parts you ever lost.

I sometimes wish to swim in the Long Beach lagoon
and get California tacos and feel all tension evaporate.
I wish our dog would never have to be called your dog.

I don't know what sunlight fixes
until it is gone. It was gone for too long.

I forgot that I am a sunlight factory.

I wondered how I would stay in this world when
the pretty death ooze of volcanoes kept calling.

I run at night when the death calls come.
Legs strong as Italian gondola oars,
drunk cars gunning for my spine.

Love is so trying.
There was a time when we were trying.

And now is a good life—
a time when I obsess about running
and nothing else.

MY LITTLE BOAT
for Dan and Sara

The only Italian song I sing well
is "Santa Lucia."

It's an invitation by an Italian boatman
to come enjoy the night in his dark boat.

On the sea it glitters (Sul mare Luccica)
The silver star (l'astro d'argento)
the wave is placid (Placida è l'onda)
prosperous is the wind (prospero è il vento)
come to me, agile (Venite all'agile)
my little boat (Barchetta mia!)
Santa Lucia. Santa Lucia!

I want to drive up on my dark motorcycle
and go to some beach or sacred spot with you and Sarah
and teach it to you both.

It makes me feel good to belt it out, sometimes in key.
You smile like a singer who doesn't like his teeth.
I like that. Let's belt the year out.

I knew the western magick and poetic shizazz
in your spirit from the day we met.

I can hear the change you carry in your pockets
for the lemonade stands.
Do you even like lemonade?

The Bixby Creek Bridge in Big Sur
was built by prisoners who worked for free
to shorten their prison sentences.

I'll wash the dishes.

You are only five hours and thirty-four minutes
of Pacific Coast Highway singing from me.

The rain shadows forth.
Henry Miller's ghost is still restless and horny.

Brautigan could have lived long here
if he wouldn't have swallowed the dark.

Orson Welles and Rita Hayworth
are moaning from the coastal redwoods.
Esalen is so naked.
I'll see you at Sand Dollar Beach
and we will dine at the Big Sur Bakery someday
and close our eyes when we eat the best grub
and say, holy shit, nothing better.

BALLAD FOR A BALLADEER

I found you when I was so broke and then didn't feel so broke
I am so sorry for making you sit through the long poetry shows
I love your voice crystallizing the sea in me so we can skate
I love your bake sale bandana, red as Springsteen's
I love that you are the end
I love that I won't have to look for you anymore
I am so tired

MURDER
for Cristin O'Keefe Aptowicz and Ernest Cline

In this part of the museum of her

you will find the diving board

she would flip wildly off at Barton Springs Pool,

under the moon we all howled to come save us at ten p.m. sharp,

and here is an audio recording of her saying "oh my stars"

under the very starlight she claimed ownership of

after she jumped into the wide, clear pool

as the water cooled the blood and the lonely-lonely,

and here is a screen capture of her face

when she walked in on her roommate Anis

pooping with the door open

only declaring one word to him:

"murder."

In this gallery are paintings of her lovely daughters

playing with my hilarious ex-girlfriend's kid

during the pandemic, best-friending it up,

and it is fine and it is lovely and those kids both rarely bathe—

the world outside looks like the trash compactor scene

from *Star Wars,*

squeezing us as we scramble for a solution.

In the loudspeakers, you will hear her singing, "stinky feet"

over and over again as the child and husband

laugh into their texan pizza.

You have to be smart to find the courage to be dumb.

In her air, you will find a hoarders obsession

of oils and diffusers revealed!

In the faces of those who turn to her, you will see them baffled

by her tireless desire to hold the lost ones

and to find their language within herself.

Do not step behind the curtain.

There is a nuclear pain that fuels this much light.

There are lunches to be made and friends to lift up

and love to accept and books to finish

and new paintings to mount.

In these watercolors,

you will notice how her husband is made out of 1985,

and he loves her madly, and his arms open silvery wide

like the doors of a Delorean.

It's such a victory that she found love.

Feel free to roam these halls wallpapered in struggle-pages,

and once you feel you know her,

drop your badges in the bin marked *fated to love her forever.*

Or at least marvel at her Scrabble skills.

See the murals of her off the exit to Philadelphia,

birds putting so much whizz on her unfazable image.

See the moment all of the world falls into a buffalo stance,

loses their mind

when she walks, or does the robot

onto the stage

and into the arms of her hollering audience,

trying to get a touch of the Philly power flowing

out of her two unknowable lanterns.

PRINCE DOESN'T NEED TO
SEE YOUR LEGS, DUDE

I was dreamin' when I wrote this;
forgive me *as it goes astray*.

I miss Prince the way a poet misses money.

I miss his JW sass, universal unisex unitard
anti-utilitarian psych-sway and swag.

When told that it was going to rain hard
during his halftime Superbowl show,
they asked Prince what he would like to do,
his reply was, "I would like . . . to know
if you could make it rain harder?"
And God said, "oh really, Gush!"

And Prince answered with the best show anyone had ever seen,
as thirty-six cheerleaders and twelve referees drowned,
Prince played on, risking electrocution and, worse,
eating shit in six-inch heels.
He never fell. Prince was a living middle finger to the heavens.

I almost got to meet him.
But a friend in my group got to Prince's house first
and he was wearing shorts, and Prince didn't allow shorts
in his house. We should have made pants out of tree bark,
or the upholstery of his backseat. Everyone left in solidarity.

I carry emergency pants in my truck now.

Dearly beloved, in 1958,
Prince Rogers Nelson wasn't born
he was c-sectioned out of an interstellar angel lust-bomb,
wished up by sex demons to kill us all with a falsetto of wonder
songs born for pussy ruin, stolen lovers,
born to shock and bonerfy a stoic world.

And what man ain't man enough to say they'd have made out with Prince?

Dearly Beloved, some of you here forgot
that you have all the magic Prince had. I mean not really, but—try.

Dearly Beloved, Never tell someone during sex that you are going to
make their pussy make sense. Let it go crazy.
Dearly Beloved, remember today that you have so much,
especially in your butt after pancakes.
Dearly Beloved, It's never a good pickup line
to tell someone you want to go down on their heart. Even at a Hot Topic.
Dearly Beloved, Sometimes it snows in April,
but remember, sledding topless is a fun challenge for shy nipples. Hubcaps out!

All hail love symbol #2; all hail the father of Manic Mondays
The Kid, The Purple Purv, The Minneapolis Midget,
Alexander Nevermind, Christopher Tracy, Skipper,
The Artist Formerly Known as Kingdom Monster,
fear-crushing genius, confident murderer of the delicate night,
middle finger to the oncoming storms of tomorrow.

To this day, nothing compares to you.

IT'S ALL COMEDY

Never watch the Glen Campbell documentary
I'll Be Me
when you are alone.

The film where Glen slowly forgets
all his songs, forgets who loves him, helpless
as a waterfall, and dies
wondering what people are.
The world is all strangers.
Why does anyone like this?

You
will cry
the Pacific.

You will wonder
why you watched that
and not *Hot Rod*.

Can't sleep. The night
holstered
by the dawn.

Who loves me?
Who loves me beyond my use?
Who loves me when I am assless
chaps at the funeral?

Frantically write down the names
of the ones who truly love you. C'mon.
Don't you wish you could fill the page?

Cry the Atlantic.
You get
what you get.

I wish I didn't know
it's all comedy.

The marionette has stumbled forward, revealing
the strings beginning to fray.
The soil beneath the stage, the hungry mouths of the dead
unglued and wide open.

Love isn't someone.
Love is a little moment.
Love is a coat that fits.

To try love on is to smile back at death,
to welcome stars as holy teeth
in the blueberry-stained mouth of night.

You will recall the pine and citrus synthetics in the shampoo smell.
Recall your hands in the wet hair of your slow exit,
when she could still look you in the eyes while inside her.

Recall the swim in the Long Beach lagoon
and how the water tasted like corn tortillas
which is not good, but you were warm and stayed in.

Recall when the searchlights of morning shined through my window
and you woke slow and I made you tea and you thanked me
and introduced yourself like it was day one. Hello, dummy. Hello, dummy.

Recall your Mother not lonely in her mind, in the endless garden.
Recall how the Sandy River water was mint
and Coors Light-cold and how the reborn forest smelled
like smoked cotton candy.

Recall the dog you adopted together
and how it was scared of the sea, the day it bolted
into the water for its first swim, confused,
scared, and then happy it got the ball. Me too. Your dog now. Cry.

Recall when you didn't live in a city
that made you weep
in the long goth gray.

Recall what sunlight fixes
until it is gone. Did I already write that?
Recall the war to remember how wanted you felt in sunlight.

Recall miles of briar and the sour blackberries among the sweet on your fingers.
Recall how the flavor that would come back when you washed the stain.

Recall the lean months
without meat or good fruit.

Recall and welcome it all.
Nothing can fuck me until
I spread. Love. Come again and fuck me up.
I remember. I'm okay with another stumble.
I remember how to get up and do shit.
I remember it all.

This
is the way
I fight
God.

ALWAYS

The Whitney version: Power wash, I'm at the edge of everything,
I cut the sky for you.

The Dolly version: Frail as a wine glass, at the limit of my skill,
mistakenly hopeful.

I'll go full Dolly on you
every time.

A GLASS BOUQUET

A bouquet
for forgetting.

Someone finally comes in,
stage left
with a handful
of softer tomorrows.

I will tell you where I'm at
and what I need.

I will not be an unsolvable maze.

I already see you
throwing flowers over your shoulder
to your lonely friends.

29 RECORDS

Bless the jasmine that roasted and died
in the dull summer
September combustion.

Bless my shaky Ikea bench
and my double-stacked seat cushion
for dining at length alone.

Bless my books that are not organized by color anymore,
looking happy and worn,
unfinished.

Bless my fake lavender plant
begging me to be watered
so it can feel real for once.

Bless my painting of a butt on my wall
that I turn to like a shrine
when the dark begs me to walk off into it.

Bless my Scholastic News Ranger Moon chart
that holds the Ocean of Storms, the Sea of Serenity,
kicking up the dust in the Sea of Nectar.

Bless the little pieces of barn wood on my wall,
that I pulled off my old ranch in Texas,
the land and love that I thought would be forever.

Bless the elephant hiding.
Bless the painting Jen did of two wrestlers in love with a trophy.
Bless the times we would look at that and say it was
our favorite thing in the house.

Bless the 30 records I have left, selling hundreds
when I moved onto a boat. Slow danced and cauterized to this one. 29 records.

Bless the gifted records I thought we
would play during dinner.
Sound of man getting record out of trash.

Bless the salt rock lamp
and how no one knows
how to explain how the damn thing is healing.

Bless the hibernating guitar
that refuses
to learn me.

Bless the air filter
for easing
the wildfire smoke.

Bless the large photograph of Catalina Island
that I long ago
decided to end my days on.

Bless the blueberries stained on the plate
from the waffles
that were just all right.

Bless the spaghetti sauce stain on the other plate
for helping me sleep
spaghetti deep.

Bless the half-bottle of Japanese whiskey
I learned to set down early,
finally. I cried last night my first sober cry.

Bless my Alf mug that says "You're one of my favorite aliens,"
and bless the person who g,ave that to me
after I devoured her cat.

Bless the picture of a framed hymnal called the Tennessee Moon,
a riverboat cruising with fog smoke steaming from its pillars,
the big wheel churning down the Mississippi where Jeff Buckley
died horny and unfinished.

Bless the Murphy's cleaning spray
that smells like the boat
that compressed and swayed the good and bad parts of me
into one.

Bless the pictures
of the paratroopers
I'll never see again.

Bless the poster of All Tomorrow's Parties and my name on it,
the moment I thought everything would change
for me.

Bless the cold water bidet.
I forsook you for too long. My little shocker.
I love any jolt that cleanses.

Bless the joy loop I am locked in
and my refusal to learn the spell
that breaks it.

NOTES

Himalayan salt lamps purify air through the power of hygroscopy, meaning that they attract water molecules from the surrounding environment then absorb those molecules—as well as any foreign particles they may be carrying—into the salt crystal. As the HS lamp warms up from the heat produced by the light bulb inside, that same water then evaporates back into the air and the trapped particles of dust, pollen, smoke, etc. remain locked in the salt. Or, magic.

ACKNOWLEDGMENTS

Thank you to these champs who helped get me to the finish line.
I owe you half my heart. The bad half.

♥

Lizzy Ellison. I love all that I learned from you. When you said you were going to get yourself a Brazilian, I was thinking something else.

I had massive edits and ideas from the genius minds of Mongo Jolley, Rebecca Gillespie, Paul Maziar, Jeremy Radin, Jessica Abughattas, Vandie, Chris Kessler, Eryn Berg, Maxwell Kessler, the beautiful wonder of Aly Sarafa, Meghan Plunk-Plunk, Chelsea Bayouth, Sam Preminger, Glenn Mobley, Olivia Gatwood, Courtney LeBlanc.

Some comedians and pals gave me advice and inspiration when I was very lost. Thank you Kyle Kinane, Eugene Mirman, Bobcat Goldthwait, David Cross, Simon Gibson, Christina Catherine Martinez, Gideon Yago and Aviva Yael. Ritch Ruiz, Shelby Pendergast, Jason Whitton- you are all my inspirados.

Thank you Amber Tamblyn for saving my life and smelling like asphalt.
Thank you Carrie Imberman for that meal when I was dead broke in New York.
Dan Esposito, your meat plate and couch was so wonderful. You know what I mean.

Emily Mundy read through my whole pile of rough work and it was no fun. I owe you so much wine. Megan Jasper and Brian. So many front rubs.
Nikki Steele has given so much to me as far as hard work and kindness. So grateful for you in my life and all you do to mamke poetry known.

Jeffrey McDaniel I got deep into this. Mindy Nettifee is my heart and champion when things get bleak. Dani and Drew McTaggart. Let me be your dog. I love you. Jordana Oberman, Jason Whitton and Sofia Fey. You give me juice! Talented, friendly juice.

Thank you Sean Casey at The Glendale Room and The Lyric Hyperion for employing m when I was in the gutter. Joel Chmara, Baz, Timmy, Robbie- Liverpool forever.

Thanks to the random woman at the nail salon that paid for my toes. Thank you Amanda Rafkin for being the best hug ever. Thanks for the deep inspiration, Sarah Kay and Clint Smith. Kelly Brown and Javier Martinez, miss you homies. Thank you to the John Wilke Kissing Booth for showing me how to nerd-out onstage. Beau Jennings, please marry me

Adrian Wyatt, you keep saving me and I am glad to still see you are married to the sea. Fucking Angelo Maneage for your lovely eye and skill at capturing fascination.

To my screenwriter pals, Scott Derrickson, Maggie Levin, Kurt Braunohler, Beth Stelling Maxwell Kessler, Ed Voccola, Chris Cullari, Ernest Cline: thank you for listening and making me feel loved during all the advice and garbage drafts.

Thank you Miles Teller for the new shoes, illusions and camping gear. I'm finally warm.

Thank you to all gondoliers, from Long Beach to Venice, for being the ghosts of romance Thank you beautiful Spencer Woolard for the ride. Brendan Constantine. My Laureate.

Thank you Diana Lee Badass Zadlo for your photos and gold laugh and strength. Thank Noyel Gallimore for your talent, glass of water and this photo of me when I was roasted o the road. Andrew Paul Nelson, Dylan Meyer and the best poets- Buddy Wakefield, Mega Falley and Andrea Gibson. You inspire the shit outta me.

Thank you to other friends and compatriots who lifted me up, Micah Bournes, Keayvah, Derek Delgaudio, The Koubas, Peter Dever, Dion Bellemare. Trish Fucking Hadley and Holly Gabrielson and Matt Kirshen. Sweetie pie city. Thank you Kaylen Krebs for the 4 month skate sesh of joy. Alexander Benavidez, Sarah Lavell, Benny Pearson, Julie Pearson you are total gifts with no return receipt.

Thank you Buzzy Enniss. You flew up to drive me back to a better life and I ate your crab when you went to the bathroom. Bruh. Forever my bruh. To Frayn Masters and Beth Lis Dream Champions. Uplift pros. Rick and Beth Redick. I love seeing your love.

Last: To The Forever Gentlemen Bosses. Anis Mojgani and Cristin O'Keefe Aptowicz. Y are my chunked up heart and the reason I keep chugging on.

Photo by Noyel Gallimore

*

Derrick C. Brown is a poet, comedian, novelist, librettist, and screenwriter. He is the founder and president of Write Bloody Publishing. He is the winner of the Texas Book of the Year prize. He was a former paratrooper for the 82nd Airborne. His poetry books include Born in the Year of the Butterfly Knife, I Love You Is Back, Scandalabra, Strange Light, Our Poison Horse, Hello. It Doesn't Matter, How the Body Works the Dark and Love Ends in a Tandem Kayak. His latest musical project is LARKK. Find out more at BrownPoetry.com and follow him on Instagram @DerrickBrownPoetry.

IF YOU LIKE DERRICK C. BROWN,
DERRICK C. BROWN LIKES...

Thin Ice Olympics
by Jeffrey McDaniel

Birthday Girl with Possum
by Brendan Constantine

How to Love the Empty Air
by Cristin O'Keefe Aptowicz

Counting Descent
by Clint Smith

Drive Here and Devastate Me
by Megan Falley

The Tigers They Let Me
by Anis Mojgani

WRITEBLOODY
QUALITY AMERICAN BOOKS

Write Bloody Publishing publishes and promotes great books of poetry every year.
We believe that poetry can change the world for the better. We are an independent press dedicated
to quality literature and book design, with an office in Los Angeles, California.

We are grassroots, DIY, gut-punch believers. Pull up a good book and join the family.
Support independent authors, artists, and presses.

Want to know more about Write Bloody books, authors, and events?
Join our mailing list at www.writebloody.com

WRITE BLOODY BOOKS

CPSIA information can be obtained
at www.ICGtesting.com
Printed in the USA
JSHW030651090323
38671JS00004B/11